D1525096

BEARDED DRAGONS

FOR BEGINNERS

A Complete Guide to Learn What a Bearded Dragon Requires to Sustain, How to Care for it and Keep Your Bearded Dragon Happy, Healthy, and Adequately Fed

By

ALEXANDER GREER

utter responsibility of the recipient reader. Under no

circumstances will any legal responsibility or blame be held against the publisher for any reparation, damages, or monetary loss due to the information herein, either directly or indirectly.

Respective authors own all copyrights not held by the publisher.

The information herein is offered for informational purposes solely and is universal as so. The presentation of the information is without a contract or any guarantee assurance.

The trademarks used are without any consent, and the trademark publication is without permission or backing by the trademark owner. All trademarks and brands within this book are for clarifying purposes only and are the owned by the owners, not affiliated with this document.

Table of Contents

Introduction

The bearded dragon or beardie is true to its name - It has armour made of sharp reptile scales, much like a dragon, and a spikey beard under its chin which changes size depending on its mood. There're 8 identified species of these dragons, also called beardies.

The kind, attentive, and the energetic bearded dragon is among the most common pet reptiles. The most popular species to keep as a pet is Pogona vitticeps, the central beardie.

The majority of Australia is included in the bearded dragon's natural range. They often favor warm, dry environments, such as subtropical forests, deserts, scrublands, and savannas. Australia outlawed exporting wild beardies in the 1960s, but they have been raised for generations in the US for the trade and are available in a range of color "morphs" uncommon in the wild.

Beardies need a warm environment. Being cold-blooded, they need outside heat sources to maintain a constant body temperature that changes depending on the ambient temperature. They may burrow below to escape excessive temperatures and attack while they bask in the sunlight to warm themselves. They often live on tree branches & fence posts and are semi-arboreal.

The beardie is not a fussy eater. Using powerful jaws, they can clasp and smash insects with shells, like beetles. They are omnivores and may sometimes eat tiny lizards or rodents in addition to flowers, fruit, and leaves.

Adult beardies, renowned for being aggressive and territorial, may battle for food, seek females, or protect their territory from other males. If females don't act subserviently, many males may assault them.

The lizards' beards, which both females & males have, are an essential part of their communication system. A beardie will push out its beard, widen its jaws, and lift its neck when it feels threatened. A hiss might also be heard along with this display.

Beardies may also converse by swaying their heads and changing the colour of its beards. While an arm wave and a leisurely head bob are signs of submission, a rapid head bob might refer to dominance.

When the seasons change, some beardies might experience brumation, a hibernation. During this period, they stop feeding and only occasionally sip water. As the seasons change and the temp drops, they often go into dormancy in the autumn or winter.

One of the easiest to care for reptiles is the bearded Dragon, so they make wonderful pets. Before introducing a certain type of animal into your house, it is essential to educate yourself on its husbandry needs, diet, substrate, and behavior, as with any other animal.

Chapter 1: Bearded Dragon Species Profile And Care Guide

Due to their obedience and propensity for adjusting to confinement, bearded dragons are sociable lizards that are accepted into any household and excellent for novices.

Bearded dragons, sometimes called "Beardies," may frequently be seen in Australia's forests and on the ground; they live in trees mostly. They are distinguished by their wide-open smiles, which are a method of cooling down.

Bearded dragons like to eat insects and green vegetables and are quite simple to care for. You may see them in confinement, soaking up the brightness or relishing the shade. They are among the most preferred reptile companions and pets since they are quite tolerant of handling.

If you're interested in this amiable reptile and wish to know how to look for these dragons and where to get them, keep reading to find out what to anticipate.

1.1 How Do Bearded Dragons Look?

Australian native bearded dragons are huge, semi-arboreal lizards that live mostly on the ground and in trees. They possess spines on each side of their bodies that extend to the bottom of their tail and may reach a length of around 15 to 20 inches, counting their tail.

Because of the skin flap beneath their chin that expands to ward off predators, these dragons got their title.

The Eight species of the genera Pogona together go by the popular name 'bearded dragons.' They were once part of the Amphibolurus genus family, but Pogona was subsequently assigned to them.

The Central Braided Dragon, also known as Pogona vitticeps, is among the most famous of the 6 species since it is friendlier and requires less upkeep than the other 5.

The popularity of bearded dragons amongst reptilian owners may be attributed to three key factors:

- Since bearded dragons are often raised in the US, several trustworthy breeders may be readily located.

- They are quite tolerant of handling and pick-up confinement pretty fast.

- Because bearded dragons are not nocturnal like some other reptile species, they are active throughout the day.

Common Names	Black-Soil Plains, Eastern, Lawson's, Kimberly, Rankin's, Western, Small-Scale, Dwarf, Nullarbor, North-West, Inland & Central Bearded Dragons
Adult Size	230-530 g, 15- 20 inches

Scientific Name	P. henrylawsoni, Pogona barbata, P. minor, P. microlepidota, P. vitticeps, P. nullarbor
Life Span	7 to 12 years
Tank Size	4x2x2 ft (minimum)
Diet	Insects & green vegetables
Other Alternatives	Crested Gecko, Blue Tongued Skinks, & Leopard Gecko

1.2 Care Guide For Bearded Dragons

The recommendations may vary somewhat based on which of the 6 species you choose since this management guide is focused on the Pogona vitticeps. The majority of the accompanying advice is suitable for all 6 species.

This lizard's natural habitat in Australia is a wooded, semi-desert landscape. Semi-arboreal in nature, bearded dragons hang out on the ground or branches.

They need very little maintenance, including:

- A heat-producing infrared light with a UVB lamp
- A 36ft³ cage with an enclosure
- A diet that includes both green vegetables and insects

Exposure And Tank

A glass container with a screening top is ideal for a bearded dragon. Their tank should be two feet broad, 4 to 6 feet long, and 2 to 3 feet tall.

This lizard can fit in a tank of this capacity and prevent the tank from scorching. Generally speaking, a larger tank is preferable.

They should have branches and rocks in the tank to provide them places to retreat and shelter to cool down after spending some time under heated lighting, which will better resemble their natural habitat.

Heating And Lighting

Bearded dragons are a diurnal lizard species, meaning they are up and active throughout the day. They must experience twelve hours of sunshine and twelve hours of nightfall.

For complete health, bearded dragons need exposure to UV radiation. A UV radiometer may be used to monitor UVB bulbs, which need to be changed every six to twelve months. They must be given a UVB bulb as well as a 40-75W infrared lamp so they can relax.

Some prefer being outdoors during the day; if you want to do this, keep an eye on your lizard!

The tank must have two climates: a "cold" side and a side for basking. To keep track of the temps on both sides, have 2 thermometers nearby:

Bearded dragons like to soak up the sun, so keep this area of their tank between 95 to 105 degrees Fahrenheit.

The temperature in the remainder of the tank ought to be around 80°F during the day, although it may drop at night. Any pebbles in the tank won't become too hot if heating pads are placed underneath it.

Their ribs will stretch in the heat to receive as much heat as possible, giving them a "flat" look.

If a bearded dragon often opens its jaws and displays an exaggerated "smile," the tank could be too warm.

By spraying the tank every two days, the moisture in the tank may be kept between 30% to 40%. Your geographic area and, eventually, the kind of Braided Dragon you keep in captivity determine the precise temperature and humidity. The humidity is generally low, while temperatures are fairly high.

Substrate

For a more genuine base, gravel or sand might be used. Sand, however, may harm your Dragon's digestive system if a bearded dragon unintentionally consumes it.

Alternatives that are safer and simpler to dispose of and clean include paper towels and newspapers. If there are any indications of bacterial development, this medium must be cleansed immediately.

Lighting	Infrared and UVB
Tank Type	Glass tank
Best Substrate	Newspaper

1.3 The Bearded Dragon's Diet

They are omnivores while living in the wild. Bearded dragons consume fruits, greens, flowers, tiny lizards, small rodents, spiders, worms, and insects.

As impulsive predators, they strike when their prey is around.

Their nutrition is simple to manage while they are in captivity.

When they are hatchlings (less than two months old), they eat two to three times daily.

Vegetables should make up 30% of the diet, while tiny insects should make up 70%. Super worms, pink mice, or crickets may provide protein in their meal. They should consume the following veggies throughout all phases of their lives:

- Dandelions
- Zucchini
- Beet tops
- Squash
- Romaine lettuce
- Leafy greens
- Carrots

Young dragons must often feed as juveniles and consume a healthy diet of insects and green vegetables. Feed insects to your pets regularly and vegetables every day.

A bearded dragon must be fed every day when it is an adult. Mainly crickets and a tonne of leafy greens like mustard and collard greens must make up this meal.

Their meals should also include vitamin D3 and calcium supplements to keep them fresh. It is recommended to serve your Dragon during the day so that it can digest it throughout the warmest portion of the day.

They are picky about their fluid intake if they must receive it from a deep container. As a result, it is advisable to constantly provide them with clean water from the shallow bowl.

1.4 How To Maintain Their Health

Consistent and proper husbandry is one of the greatest

strategies to maintain your bearded Dragon's health.

It's not necessary to bathe your Dragon; however, immersing him in lukewarm water twice a week can encourage feces production. They shed in many chunks over a few days. Diet and season affect how often they shed.

They are more inclined to shed their skin when they routinely feed in the summer and spring. Near the fingers and tail tip, there may be any unusual shedding. If this occurs, they might need a bath to prevent an infection.

Upkeep Of Their Tank

You should completely replace and remove the substrate weekly while cleaning their aquarium. Sand is harder to replenish than paper towels and newspaper.

Weekly cleanings of the tank with diluted soap and water are recommended.

Daily spot cleaning is required if the substrate contains old food, waste, or water that has been spilled. You should inspect and clean up your Dragon's excrement, looking for anomalies. The typical feces of a bearded dragon ought to be pelleted, brown, and include a semisolid urate.

You should take your Dragon to the veterinarian if the excrement seems odd or if you spot any blood. This might be an indication of an endoparasitic illness.

What Is The Lifespan Of Bearded Dragons?

In captivity, beardies last between 7 - 12 years. They make reasonably healthy pets, and most bearded dragon health problems result from poor management.

A lack of UVB sunshine, a phosphorus imbalance in the diet, and a calcium shortage might cause metabolic bone disease. Your Dragon drooping its limbs, tail, or torso rather than standing up straight is a sign of this illness.

When dragons are kept together, cage aggressiveness may potentially cause trauma. This species is less prone to cardiac and renal disorders and intestinal impaction, often caused by ingesting substrate.

1.5 Signs Of Good Health

- Delighted to bask

- Will flee if you attempt to capture them

- The Dragon rises tall and high on all 4 limbs, his muscles well-rounded.

Symptoms Of Illness

- Using voice to express distress

- Limiting oneself to the sunbathing area

- Random loss of weight

- Not wanting to eat

1.6 Behavior Of A Bearded Dragon

This type of lizard is known for its propensity for aggression in its native environment, which is the wild. They will establish a social hierarchy with one dominating lizard if several reside in the same location. They might clash, pursue, or even mount one another. The most friendly lizard in the species will become the dominant one, and they often engage in competitive behavior.

For nourishment, bearded dragons will engage in combat. They accomplish this by circumducting or swaying their heads and rotating their legs. They would also exchange heated looks with one another.

Their "beard" will grow out to make them seem intimidating and much larger if they perceive a threat, whether by a predator or dominant Dragon.

Even though bearded dragons are quite friendly to people, they may exhibit similar behavior in captivity if kept with other dragons. It is better to avoid housing these reptiles alongside since they will establish a social order and may even become hostile.

Bearded dragons are content and amiable reptiles when left alone. Although they will sometimes conceal, they are comfortable and often switch between their sunbathing location and the shade.

Bearded dragons may have a brumation phase when they feed sporadically less often and slumber for 2 to 4 months. Many breeders will brumate their dragons before allowing them to mate. This may be done by maintaining the tank's temperature between 60°F to 75°F for four to six weeks, then gradually raising it afterward.

Handling

The tail may come off but won't grow back. Therefore, you shouldn't ever grab them, even by the tail.

Always rinse your hands before touching your Dragon and after that. Generally speaking, this helps to stop the spread of germs like Salmonella. Beardies are highly obedient to humans.

Although they could flee at first when you attempt to capture them, they are quite good at handling and might even be pleased to rest on your shoulder.

They will feel more secure if you carry them flat rather than cradling them. Give your new Dragon 3 to 4 days to become used to you before trying to handle them for brief periods.

Appearance

Beardies have thick tongues, spherical pupils, and transverse spines extending from the tail's bottom down their flanks.

They have triangular-shaped heads that are big and wide. Additionally, they have beards that swell and act as a protection mechanism if they sense danger. Furthermore, your pet's head bobbing may indicate feeling threatened, apprehensive, or uncomfortable.

Male bearded dragons often have more pronounced patterns and darker colors than females. They often have a broader tail base as well.

Size

The length of a bearded dragon ranges from 15 - 20 inches. Beginner herpetologists would think this is a huge deal, but their snout-to-vent length is just ten inches. Within 18 to 24 months, a baby should weigh approximately 230 to 520g, which is the weight of an adult.

The colors range from orange to brown based on the morph and species. Although pastel lizards get silute pigmentation, sandfire morphs are more closely related to a red hue. Some are said to appear in yellow as well.

There are a few particular lineages that are cultivated in captivity to have certain appearances:

- The Leatherback has been bred to have smaller scales.

- The Silk back was bred to be completely scaleless.

1.7 Babies Of A Bearded Dragon

A masculine bearded dragon would darken his neck and circle a female to attract her. She will lower her body to permit copulation if she agrees. The male may bite a female's throat during copulation. Such mating occurs in the early summer and spring when the female's progesterone levels are highest. It is advisable to brumate your lizards before breeding them since this occurs after brumation.

As household Bearded Dragons lay their eggs, a nesting box must be supplied; however, a space with soil or sand that is 10 inches deep would work just fine. Female grizzled dragons, unlike other reptiles, will produce 3 clutches of up to thirty-five eggs each.

The eggs must be taken from the nesting box after the female lays them and placed in an incubator with vermiculite soil and water replacer at 82°F to 86°F; the eggs will develop in 3 to 4 weeks.

The egg tooth is a tool babies use to pry themselves out of their shells. Dragons should be separated from one another as soon as they hatch because they may establish a social structure similar to that of adults.

If a novice herpetologist decides to buy a Beardie (rather than breeding one), they should opt for a reptile between three and six months old. They are currently developing and eating often.

For novices, the amiable bearded Dragon is a fantastic lizard. They have placid temperaments that make them manageable and reasonably simple to care for. They're also adored for their distinct personalities & smiling looks.

Few reptiles can compete with this Dragon for a place in reptilian owners' imaginations. The Leopard Gecko is another excellent starter reptile.

The Blue Tongued Skink & Crested Gecko are two lizards that might be harder to manage. While not nearly as chatty as a Bearded Dragon, these creatures don't need as much warmth or light.

Overall, beardies are calm reptiles with a simple diet. They need lighting and warmth, but with the right arrangement, these are readily accessible.

Make it a family member by picking one to carry home with you!

Chapter 2: A Quick Guide To Bearded Dragon Life

2.1 Bearded Dragon: Temperament, Traits, & Origin

One of the easiest to care for reptiles is the bearded Dragon, so they make wonderful pets. Before selecting to introduce a certain type of animal into your house, it is essential to educate yourself on its husbandry needs, as with any other animal. Let's begin by being acquainted with the Dragon's history.

Member of the lizard family "Agamidae," bearded dragons are indigenous to Australia's outback. They have a recognizable large, triangular-shaped skull and a generally flat body; their mouths and torsos are covered with scales resembling thorns. Adults reach a length of 18 to 24 inches, along with the tail. Typically, males are substantially larger than females.

Supplies needed for a bearded dragon include:

- A cage (minimum of the thirty-gallon breeding tank)
- Screen top with wire mesh
- Items for decorations
- A hide box
- Fluorescent light bulb (full-spectrum) with protected fixture for reptiles
- Ceramic heat emitters or heat lamps with dome-shaped fittings
- Heat pad
- Pebbles or driftwood for a perch
- Water and food bowls
- Minimum of 2 mercury or digital thermometers

Australian Species Distribution

Distribution of Pogona in Australia

1. Pogona Barbata
2. Pogona Henry Lawsoni
3. Pogona Minor Minor
4. Pogona Minor Minima
5. Pogona Minor Mitchelli
6. Pogona Microlepidota
7. Pogona Nullarbor
8. Pogona Vitticeps

2.2 The Reasons Bearded Dragons Make Great Pets

The popularity of bearded dragons among enthusiasts & pet owners has increased recently. They are now the most in-demand lizard pet on the market, surpassing iguanas. Below are some of their wonderful features, which explain why they are such well-liked pets:

Calm Behavior: They are well known for their peaceful disposition and playful nature; they are gentle, if not downright obedient, animals. Once they become acquainted with their owners, it is rare to find any who don't like being snapped up and cuddled. One reason lizards were becoming such a well-liked pets is their fantastic attitude, which makes it extremely simple to establish a strong bond with them.

Very Easy To Maintain: Unlike most lizards sold as pets, dragons are incredibly simple to care for. Additionally, they do not have as specific nutritional requirements as other lizards. Raising a bearded dragon is simple as long as you spend a little time properly cleaning and maintaining its environment daily.

Distinctive Look: This species' aesthetic is among its most alluring qualities. They come in various colors and have a fascinating, dinosaur-like appearance. They are widely available in pastel colors and orange, yellow, and red tones. One of their appealing traits is their bushy beard.

Tiny Size: Adult dragons have a height of 8- 24 inches, considered small. Pet owners find them appealing because of their diminutive size, making managing and keeping them much simpler.

Long Lifespan: When grown in captivity, it's not improbable that they may survive up to fifteen years old. Another appealing aspect of theirs is their robust health since they're not as delicate as numerous other reptiles, such as turtles or chameleons.

2.3 Finding a Healthy Dragon

- Has a taste for both vegetables and insects.

- Clear, attentive eyes.

- Active, not sluggish.

- Region and clean.

- No lacerations and lumps on the skin.

- Mouth and mouth are normal, with no drooping or deformity.

- Complete tail.

- Good pigmentation, no dark or damaged regions.

- Healthy-Bearded

- 5 toes/foot, with claws.

2.4 What To Look For In A Healthy-Bearded Dragon

It's time to choose a bearded dragon after you've determined that it's the ideal pet for you. This is a really important stage. It would help if you never bought a sick or diseased dragon. Although it is simple to feel sympathy for an ill or injured newborn bearded dragon, it can be challenging for a novice to restore it to health. When selecting your Dragon, keep the following in mind:

Check Out The Habitat: Most young, bearded dragons are obtained from pet shops, although many are also available through breeders. The first thing you should do when choosing an animal from a pet shop is looking at the environment. Make sure it is clean and well-kept, with no leftover food or feces. Examine the environment to check whether it is overpopulated. It is significantly crowded when twenty to thirty infants are kept in a single ten-gallon habitat. Injuries like damaged and broken toes or tails may result from an overcrowded environment. Verify that the pet shop has a bathing area with enough heat for the infants and light-emitting UV-B rays.

Watch The Bearded Dragons: Take a close look at the actual bearded dragons. Please take a seat back and observe them for a while. It would help if you chose a particularly active and vigilant pet. Examine how the habitat responds when you wave your finger in front of it. They should fix their attention on the action carefully. While some dragons may leap at sudden movements, most will observe with some interest. A bearded dragon that is awake, engaged, and seems to be feeding well is what you want. Avoid those that seem frail and thin.

2.5 How To Examine Your Dragon's Basic Health

When you've found a specimen that fits your requirements, ask a shop employee to remove it from its environment so you may examine it more closely. The bearded Dragon must be lively and might at first wiggle a little. Ensure you have a firm grip on it without holding it too tightly. Keep in mind the following:

- Check the eyes. Once again, check to see whether they're clear and awake and if there is any crust in their eyes or mouth.

- Verify the integrity of the feet and toes. Each foot must have 5 toes, each of which should possess the complete claw. Check to see whether the toes are not swollen or malformed.

- Verify that the tail is whole and not damaged or misshapen. Check the whole body for bumps, bruises, and lacerations. To check whether the skin is in excellent form and feels fresh, pat it. The skin should still be somewhat elastic.

- Turn the reptile over and look at the abdomen. It shouldn't have bumps or abrasions and must be off-white to white.

- Check the anal area; it should be free of clumps or residual fecal material.

2.6 Dietary And Nutritional Needs

Even though dragons have diverse appetites and palates, there are several things to keep in mind while providing well-balanced food. Lizards need a diversified, balanced meal with plenty of minerals and vitamins since their nutritional requirements change as they mature.

Baby Bearded Dragon Nutrition

Bearded dragons are considered juveniles until they are 4 to 5 months old. The baby will develop quickly at this time and needs nourishment and minerals. A variety of bug feeders & finely cut veggies should be provided to infants. Bug feeders must make up 60- 80%of their diet, while various vegetables should compensate for 20 - 40 percent.

Per meal, give the bearded Dragon 3 to 4 pinhead crickets. Babies must be given little, frequent meals throughout the day to support their fast development. Instead of serving them one huge meal per day, it is preferable to provide them with 3 to 4 smaller ones. Since wax worms are heavy in fat and can induce obesity later in life, avoid giving them too many. A good place to start is by providing 1 or 2 wax worms every day.

Don't give newborn mealworms. Mealworms may have a tough outer layer that is challenging for a newborn to digest. Don't distribute excessively big crickets. The cricket's spiky hind legs may tear the fragile digestive tract of newborns.

Minerals And Vitamins

Vitamin D3 and calcium supplements should be included in each meal while feeding a newborn bearded dragon to encourage strong bone development and growth. It is crucial to provide essential minerals and vitamins to continue their fast development throughout the newborn.

A Tip On Feeding Young Bearded Dragons Vegetables

Make sure the veggies are properly chopped since this is crucial. Provide the baby dragon with a well-balanced meal and a range of veggies.

- Kale

- Endive

- Dandelions

- Yellow squash

- Collards

- Turnip greens

- Escarole

- Watercress

- Sweet potato

- Carrots

- Mustard greens

- Green peas

Baby Dragon Fruit Feeding Instructions

Give your bearded Dragon a variety of fruits and veggies each day. Its appetite for fruits and vegetables will develop as a result.

- Diced apples

- Seedless grapes

- Diced pears

- Diced pineapple

- Orange chunks

Diced kale is the best food for young, adult, and newborn bearded dragons.

Note: Never give your bearded dragons food bigger than the distance between their eyes.

Providing Food For A Young-Bearded Dragon

When a dragon is between the ages of 5 to 18 months, it is referred to as a juvenile. You should gradually reduce the number of bug feeders while increasing the number of mixed vegetables and fruits supplied during this period in the reptile's life. Insect feeder varieties will also expand. The size of the available insects may also be increased.

Listed below are various insects you may give a youngster:

- Mealworms

- fruit flies

- crickets

- wax worms

- roaches

- super worms

The proportion of insect feeders supplied should decline to around 40% throughout the adolescent stage of life, while the proportion of vegetables and fruits provided should rise to about 60%. A tiny giving of bug feeders & 2 small vegetable presentations may be given to juveniles per day.

Minerals And Vitamins

The supplement may be lowered to a sprinkle every other day after it enters the juvenile stage.

Feeding A Bearded Dragon Adult

The meal schedule for adults differs from that of infants and young dragons. Adults need fewer insect presenters and more green vegetables. When a bearded dragon is eighteen months, its meal should be made up of 80% fruits and vegetables and 20% insect eaters.

Adults must be given a substantial dose of leafy greens and chopped veggies like sweet potatoes, green peas, and carrots about two times a day. Reduce the frequency of the bug feeders to 2 to 3 times each week. Adults need less fat and protein than infants, and young children do.

Minerals And Vitamins

Each week, adults may get a broad-spectrum multivitamin to help them get the extra minerals and vitamins they need at this point.

Vegetable Feeding Instructions

- Kale

- Mustard greens

- Red cabbage

- Green peas

- Collard greens

- Dandelions

- Escarole

- Carrots

- Arugula

- Okra

- Endive

- Parsley

- Bell peppers

- Squash

- Watercress

- Alfalfa sprouts

- Green beans

Fruit Feeding Instructions

- Pears

- Papaya

- Mango

- Grapes

- Strawberry

- Apples

- Pineapple

- Kiwi

- Orange Slices

2.7 Housing For Bearded Dragons

Once you've decided to acquire a bearded dragon, you'll need to provide suitable accommodation. A cheerful, vibrant lizard must have the proper environment.

The Container

- Determine the kind of enclosure you'll be using. On the marketplace, there are numerous different kinds of tanks and terrariums built specifically for hosting reptiles. For a unique appearance, you might even construct your enclosure. It is recommended to start with an enclosure that is big enough to contain an adult.

- Because bearded dragons are free-roaming creatures and not great climbers, it's best to choose an enclosure with plenty of floor space to avoid purchasing new ones as they become bigger. Use a breeder tank that is no less than 30 gallons. Thirteen inches tall, eighteen inches broad, and thirty-six inches long make up this tank. The nicer an enclosure is, the more floor space it offers.

Acrylic vs. Glass

- Given their affordability and ease of upkeep, glass terrariums are among the greatest choices. There are also acrylic-built terrariums. Though significantly thinner than glass, acrylic enclosures have also far more scratch-prone. Ensure a wire mesh screen (snug-fitting) cover to prevent other animals from leaving your Dragon's house. Glass lids should not be used as they will block necessary UV-B rays from the illumination.

- Substrate: The habitat's floor is covered with the substrate. A contentious issue in the dragon world is the substrate. Several owners use newspapers since it is simpler to maintain, whereas many homeowners use organic non-silica sand to provide a more realistic environment. You may use whatever is necessary, but to prevent impaction, stay away from substrates with minute particles. When a lizard consumes something it can't digest, it experiences impaction, which obstructs the intestines. Avoid using stones, aquarium rocks, powdered walnut shells, & anything else that might easily result in an impaction. This can be lethal unless it is identified promptly and treated by a veterinarian. In particular, this is true of young bearded dragons.

Enhancing The Environment

- **Furnishings And Plants:** You may add furnishings and plants to spice up the environment. The best choice is to use silk or plastic plants. They are less likely to be swallowed by your bearded Dragon, are simple to clean, and do not require water. Ensure any live plants you choose are chemical-free and won't harm your pet before buying them. To make habitat rearrangement simpler, keep live plants in a tiny container at all times.

- Bearded dragons require a **hide box**. In pet shops, there are various hide boxes to choose from. These hide boxes, which are made to resemble rock caverns, are a wonderful asset to the habitat.

- **Perching**: Among the bearded Dragon's favorite activities is perching in the bathing area. Pet retailers have a wide variety of sandblasted driftwood items. Check to see whether it can sustain your Dragon.

2.8 Lighting And Heating Requirements

The survival of your little Dragon must provide it with the right warmth and lighting. Because this species originated in Australia's scorching desert areas, it is crucial to replicate those conditions as closely as possible. They rest on stones and other natural objects while soaking up the sun's warm beams. While in confinement, trying to mimic this habitat as closely as possible is crucial.

Make Cooling And Soaking Areas

- For their offspring, bearded dragons require a warm basking surface that is 95 to 100 °F and 90 to 95 °F for grownups. To provide the ideal basking temperatures, use ceramic heat transmitters, heating lamps, and heating pads. In certain circumstances, a mix of these could be required. Do not use hot rocks as a source of heat. Hot pebbles are not advised since they are notorious for resulting in belly burns.

- A colder area should be established and maintained between 80 and 87 °F. If it becomes too warm in the bathing area, they will retreat to the cool area to relax a little. The lizard's health depends on maintaining a temperature differential across the environment.

- Keep a mercury or digital thermometer within the colder section and the bathing area to track temperatures regularly and make adjustments as necessary.

UV-B And UV-A Rays Supply

- Sunlight's UV-A and UV-B rays are also essential. Although the sun naturally produces these rays, a residence could not have them. To mimic UV-B & UV-A rays, a full-spectrum lamp especially made for reptiles would be needed.

- To help with the production of calcium and vitamin D3, which are required for healthy bone formation, UV-B rays are crucial. It's thought that UV-A contributes to the production of hormones and appetites.

- Replace light bulbs (full-spectrum) every 6 months to ensure they get enough UV A and UV-B radiation.

Prepare The Habitat For Your Bearded Dragon In Advance

To lessen the possibility of anxiety and shock, have all lighting, heating, & décor fixed at least one week before taking your dragon house. Never take a dragon house without providing food, heat, and UV lighting. Switch it all on to check that all the machinery is working correctly.

Switch on the heat emitters, heat pads, & ceramic heat sources, and keep an eye on the temps in the cooling & basking areas. Ensure they're at a level that is desired.

Ensure that the wood, substrate, plants, hide box, and rock perches, are all set up and ready to start. Before you pick up your Dragon from the pet store, put a dish with diced fruits and veggies in the habitat. A shallow water bowl should also be available.

Take Pleasure In Your Dragon's Presence

Bearded dragons are excellent pets. You won't have any trouble maintaining one of the funniest and most fascinating pets conceivable with a little care and a great deal of affection.

The Age Of My Bearded Dragon

Obtaining detailed info from the owner is the most effective approach to determining your beardie's age. Every dedicated beardie breeder keeps track of their babies and records the precise dates when the beardies hatched.

If the data isn't available for whatever reason, you'll have to make an educated guess depending on your beardie's physical characteristics. You should be aware that a neglected bearded dragon may be elder than he seems to be if you purchase one.

Beardies' sexual features will also start to emerge around the time they become twelve months old. Your bearded dragon is currently between 8 and 12 months old if you see any of these traits (bulges well above the femoral pores & cloacal entrance).

Without further information, it is impossible to accurately determine a beardie's age if they have already grown to adult size.

2.9 Bearded Dragon Behavior And Health

It's fascinating to see the communication and conduct of bearded dragons. These actions are not being taken randomly; each has a purpose. You may rapidly learn the deeper meanings behind their amusing arm waving, spastic movements, and other beardie antics with a little focus and some excellent reading.

But it's not all simply for entertainment. The best way to determine whether your bearded dragon is feeling well is to pay attention to his behavior. Certain habits may indicate that your beardie's surroundings or health need attention.

The following is a list of typical bearded dragon behaviors:

- Arm waving, head nodding, and other signals of dominance and submission

- Fear/aggression: hissing, bulging and darkened beard, biting

- In response to temperature, the animal's tail points upward, and its body becomes black.

- Another typical action is yawning.

Symptoms of the illness include lethargy, closed eyelids, hind limb paralysis, extended mouth flapping, a black beard without an external stimulus, a persistent black color while at repose, gazing (looking up at nothing in particular), twitching, and convulsions.

Brumation symptoms may sometimes be confused for illnesses. It could be appropriate for your generally healthy bearded dragon to take a winter nap if he seems lethargic, won't eat, or hides a lot in the late fall or winter.

You shouldn't be caught off guard by brumation; instead, you ought to be ready for it by putting on weight before the end of the fall and getting your beardie to the doctor for a parasite exam.

2.10 Habitat For Bearded Dragons

Wood, glass, or plastic are all acceptable materials for bearded dragon aquariums. Nevertheless, there are a few guidelines that any beardie enclosure must adhere to:

- There should be enough lighting throughout the enclosure, including both UVB & ordinary light.

- The temp must range from 70°F to 110°F at the highest.

- Humidity levels should always be maintained below 60 percent.

- Beardies should have a spot to hide, climb, and soak up the sun.

- Keeping bearded dragons on reptile carpets, paper towels, rock slates, or ceramic tiles is safer than keeping them on loose substrates like crushed walnut & sand, which may lead to impaction and other health problems. If you still want a natural substrate, these bioactive compounds are safer and provide additional advantages.

Here is some extra guidance on housing beardies that pertains to beardies themselves:

- Never put 2 males in the same residence.

- Never put an adult as well as a child in the same house.

- 2 females can usually get along, but you should keep a close eye on their interactions and have a backup tank handy just in case. The same is true for female-male relationships.

2.11 Care For Baby-Bearded Dragons

Baby dragon care differs from what you'd provide to an adult bearded dragon.

Before he enters juvenile age, you must make sure that your young beardie:

- Gets approximately 70 percent of his nourishment from insect meals but not from super worms, mealworms, or waxworms.

- Despite not being a huge fan of vegetables, he eats his vegetables.

- Regular misting keeps him hydrated.

- Obtains the optimal UVB illumination - Using a UV meter to adjust your bulb is the best option to determine if radiation levels are sufficient.

Additionally, you must make sure that:

- His length and weight are regularly recorded; completing our growth charts is the easiest way to accomplish this.

- So after feeding, there aren't any feeder bugs left in the cage since crickets may harm or even kill young dragons!

- Even if you want to raise an adult bearded dragon that way, you must never raise a newborn beardie there.

2.12 What Is The Price Of A Bearded Dragon?

Typically, a young juvenile or classic baby bearded dragon prices range from $30 to $60. Adults often cost $100 or less.

There are a good variety of distinct bearded dragon morphs available nowadays. Based on the beardie's appearance and genetics, costs may change. The price of the specimen increases with the rarity of the morph as well as the saturation of the colors. Some uncommon hybrids' adults may go upwards of $1000.

2.13 What Stores Sell Bearded Dragons

Any reptile You purchase should always be made straight from the breeder. Undoubtedly, going into a pet shop and purchasing an animal is simple. The circumstances for pets in shops are not ideal, even though every store is unique. That raises the possibility of getting a sick or underweight beardie.

Finding the best breeder for bearded dragons will take additional time and investigation. Don't only depend on their online presence. Find out a breeder's popularity by asking around, emailing your inquiries, or requesting a phone call, then attempting to base your decision on that.

Finding a local breeder is recommended so you can attend their facilities and see how the animals are cared for; it's also much preferable to scoop up your beardie in the site rather than having him sent to you. A compassionate breeder also would likely provide you with greater information and guidance than a neighborhood pet shop, and you'll have somebody to turn to if you encounter any problems.

An alternative to purchasing a bearded dragon is to acquire one from a reptile rescue facility or an animal sanctuary.

2.14 Selecting A Bearded Dragon

Always choose bearded dragons that are vibrant, huge, bright-eyed, plump, and have thick tails.

Out of sympathy, some individuals like tiny, thin, beardie kids. Even while doing this kind of "rescue" is a great deed, a novice owner should avoid doing so. The newborn dragon may have a difficult health problem that will be expensive and tedious to treat. Additionally, if you've other beardies living in your house, you run the chance of them contracting atadenovirus or parasites from their sad housemate.

It may be a good idea to bring a buddy or ask a reputable breeder for assistance, as 2 eyes are preferable to one at spotting possible problems.

Additionally, be aware that some pet stores offer newborn bears that are too premature. Always try to get a dragon that has already professionally grown up to the age of 3 months.

2.15 How Can A Bearded Dragon Be Trained?

Your bearded dragon's level of tameness will vary depending on his age or past experiences.

Baby beardies are highly timid and afraid; they dislike being touched excessively and particularly dislike being held in a closed hand.

While the infant is still little and vulnerable, the first step is to accustom him to your existence. Read a book, or converse with him while seated where he will see you. Along with giving him food, you will also quickly convince him that you're a buddy.

You may gently hold the newborn dragon without removing him from the tank after a few days of doing so. He will eventually learn to appreciate the warmth and softness of your hands.

Whenever you begin removing your newborn beardie from his tank is entirely up to you. Typically, it'll be safe to bring him outside and get him entirely used to being handled and going about secure areas when he is six months old and eleven inches tall.

Important Handling Guidelines

It's crucial to manage your bearded dragon correctly when you wish to:

- Hands should be washed properly.

- Approach quietly and gradually, keeping an eye out for any aggressive cues. It is advisable to let your bearded dragon alone until he's prepared to be touched once again if you see them.

- Gently massage his head and back until you sense that he is unwinding.

- Put one palm on the dragon's body, while the other should be placed over his armpits or shoulders.

- Note that whether your lizard is perched on your hand or your shoulder, he must always feel reassured from underneath. Never lift him by placing just one hand & letting him dangle there.

Additionally, when handling your pet, you must remain above a comfortable and secure surface, like a mattress or a couch. Your bearded dragon's fall to the floor might result in spinal damage or even death.

2.16 How Should I Interact With My Beardie?

Unlike dogs and cats, bearded dragons don't need playtime. However, a beardie must be physically and psychologically active to be fit, which is difficult to do in his tank alone. Because of this, you may plan innovative practices to keep him engaged and strengthen your relationship.

- You may easily find a beardie to read with since we will appreciate just hanging around and taking in your warmth.

- The greatest activity for your bearded dragon is a stroll around a grassy meadow that is secure and devoid of poisonous plants, pesticides, and predators. Having him strapped into a comfy reptile leash is important to stop him from running away or hiding in awkward locations.

- A bearded dragon enjoys swimming in the lovely, warm water since it aids digestion and keeps him hydrated.

- Some beardies like to investigate items with vivid colors, such as balls. You may give your bearded dragon a ball that is just the right size to roll about but not so huge that he can ingest it.

Despite the many pieces of advice and movies that claim beardies "like" vehicle drives and "modifications of scenery," We don't encourage this behavior, at least for most beardies.

Bearded dragons, like other lizards, are aggressive. Thus they get nervous and irritated when they find themselves in an unexpected location. When you bring your bearded dragon into an unfamiliar area, you'll discover that he is readily disturbed or startled by even the slightest indication of danger. Because of this, We would refrain from constantly bringing him somewhere new.

It's more enjoyable for a beardie's owner to ride along than for the lizard. There is occasionally a fine line between making your pet busy and causing him to worry.

You can take him to an area he is already comfortable with, like a backyard.

Remember to wait until your beardie is six months old before handling and playing with him excessively. Keep the conversation short and undemanding up to that age.

Therefore, Are Bearded Dragons Excellent Pets?

Beardies may be kept healthy and happy for a very long time by adhering to a few simple guidelines. Additionally, it will assist you in developing a wonderful rapport with him. Nothing about beardies is particularly challenging, yet many experiences are satisfying.

To acquire a full understanding of the ideal beardie care, keep on reading this guide.

Do you think our examination of beardies was helpful? Do you already possess a bearded dragon, or are you just getting one now? Do you have any more queries you wish to see addressed? We will answer all your queries in the next chapters.

Chapter 3: What Is The Ideal Tank Setup For A Bearded Dragon Ecosystem?

Do you have questions concerning the substrate, heating, lighting, or tank type that should be used in your beardie's enclosure? In this chapter, you may learn how to create the optimal home for bearded dragons.

As you may know, bearded dragons like walking outdoors and are best at ease in vivaria that mimic a desert environment. Additionally, despite being solitary creatures, several films depict beardies coexisting peacefully.

The situation is not, however, as simple as it initially seems.

Do you realize that:

Too many walks in strange places may distress your dragon; numerous beardies require huge enclosures, in particular, to be housed together securely; and while desert settings are best for beardies, possessing sand as a foundation can be downright harmful.

Given all the possibilities and problems floating around the internet, what is the best-bearded dragon arrangement?

Let's attempt to learn! We've compiled the greatest information on the subject so you may provide your pet with the environment he deserves.

Natural Habitat Of The Bearded Dragon

The beardie may be found in Australia's desert regions, where greenery is sparse, and the soil is largely made up of hardened, dry soil, rock, and some loose sand and soil. While diverse flora isn't very abundant, there're still numerous desert plants and tiny trees that are good for climbing and hiding under.

Water is rare, yet when it does collect, it is well used. That explains why beardies like soaking.

3.1 Types Of Container For The Bearded Dragon Tank

The ideal terrarium for a bearded dragon in confinement is a desert-themed one based on what we can learn about their native home.

It should be noted that not every component of a standard desert vivarium arrangement is suitable for beardies, particularly the young ones. Nevertheless, if you do not go overboard with intricate desert-themed decorations & sand substrate, you should still adhere to the following principles:

Beardies like the heat.

- Minimal humidity. To breathe somewhat dry air, beardies have developed. Your pets' lungs may suffer fatal pulmonary illness from high humidily levels (over 65 percent).

- A light over their tank is preferred and necessary for beardies since it will maintain their warmth and awake. Additionally, they need a second UV lighting since your pet's correct metabolism & bone formation depends on UVB and UVA radiation.

Bearded Dragon Tank Type And Size

Your bearded dragon's age & size will determine the tank's dimensions.

If you acquire a juvenile, you must keep him in a more compact, basic setting until he matures.

With adults, you might choose to put up a whole, sizable desert vivarium. Despite their average size, adult beardies are still fairly large and energetic. Thus, they require terrariums that are huge.

Juvenile Confinement

Your dragon will be kept in a juvenile cage until he reaches full maturity. A twenty-gallon tank is sufficient for little infants.

What do you require to house your tiny beardie?

- Simple substrate (paper towels, tiles, newspapers)
- A conventional heat bulb inside a clamp lamp
- A glass tank (twenty to fifty gallons)
- A fluorescent UV light
- A basking rock
- A mesh top for the terrarium is also required
- A single ascending branch

- A shallow water dish (baby dragons may quickly drown)

Below, you'll find further information about each of these elements.

Keep juvenile cages as simple as possible, as this will stop crickets and other food insects from escaping from your pet. Later, as you are setting up his adolescent cage, you may go crazy with the decorations.

Bearded Dragon Tank Design

Did you realize that the container may be composed of many materials, some of which are more suitable for beardies than others?

Let's explore the several tanks that may be used to house a bearded dragon.

Glass Terrariums

Another favorite is glass tanks. They are very visible and simple to clean. They are less likely to be scratched than plastic tanks. Nevertheless, you will require a rather big cage for mature bearded lizards, with the recommended capacity being 120 gallons. From this perspective, let's discuss a few problems that might arise if you solely utilize a glass tank.

First, a glass tank is more likely to shatter the bigger it is.

Second, a bigger tank would cost you much more than a tiny one, primarily because a bigger tank requires thicker glass.

Purchasing used glass tanks from fishkeepers is the best method to save costs on these tanks. They might be reasonably priced if you can locate them. You won't be concerned about the potential leak because you won't refill it with water. Check whether the tank has a significant fracture since this will only worsen with time.

Plastic Enclosures

Plastic containers have changed significantly over the last two decades, transitioning from basic plastic crates to sophisticated, professional enclosures.

ABS or PVC plastics are often used to construct these pre-made lizard habitats. In most cases, the front side is constructed from a transparent, plexiglass-like material; the remaining sides are dark. Although some people perceive this as a drawback in viewing, your pet may feel safer in this kind of enclosure.

In addition to being less likely to shatter than glass tanks, these also allow you to be predrilled for cables, making the entire system more aesthetically pleasing.

The difficulty with plastic containers is that they're also quite costly, particularly the 1-piece molded cage like Vision cages, which have built-in structural systems and other practical modifications. Searching for a plastic tank made in a DIY manner is more economical.

Wooden Architecture

Let's face it, constructing a sizable glass tank or purchasing a sizable prefabricated plastic container of at least 100 gallons may become pricey.

Wooden enclosures could be a good choice for those who don't like plastic, like doing DIY projects or want to reduce cost.

Using a wooden cabinet as a biosphere is also a clever idea. You might construct a wooden tank or purchase one online. Breeders commonly use this to save housing expenses for the numerous pets they must house in different facilities.

Wooden tanks are made similarly to plastic ones. The front of a wooden cage, often a glass door design, will typically be the only part not constructed of wood.

One significant disadvantage of utilizing wood is that it is permeable and absorbs moisture, making it vulnerable to decaying and fungus.

Since desert enclosures are often dry, you could assume this isn't a problem. But reconsider; you need to spritz your dragon, and he'll splash in the water bowl. All of this will be absorbed by the wood, with contaminants that will make it smell not very good and be challenging to clean.

Applying a waterproof, non-toxic coating over the whole timber surface will solve this problem. It will become smooth and water-resistant and have a lovely, shiny appearance. However, remember that it could be difficult to obtain items of this caliber, particularly cheaply.

3.2 The Preferred Lighting Setup

Almost every reptile tank must have the Best Lighting, a crucial component. Proper illumination is important for your dragon's health and provides a spectacular view of your beardie and his surroundings.

Bearded dragons require their whole cage to be lighted up to feel at home since they are diurnal lizards and are often exposed to the hot Australian sun.

The second crucial factor is UVB and UVA rays, which are essential for your pet's ability to synthesize Vit D and the healthy operation of all metabolic processes, such as the absorption of calcium and the development of strong bones.

A standard incandescent bulb in a simple, reasonably priced lamp and a complementary UV fluorescent bulb in a conventional casing make an excellent combo for young dragons. These two items fit within your mesh lid. The system's low cost, especially in comparison to mercury-vapor lights, and the possibility that you may utilize them for your adolescent cage later are benefits.

UVB Lighting

Most terrariums employ linear fluorescent bulbs as their primary source of UVB illumination. The highest grade, 10.0, is required for bearded dragons; the UV lamp of your choosing must provide 5 to 7% of UVB/A radiation and should cover 80 percent of their area.

Juvenile beardies need adequate UVB to develop strong bones and prevent the danger of metabolic, degenerative disease because of how quickly they grow. A full-spectrum lamp is ideal, although it should be noted that UVB is the essential kind of ultraviolet light and, thus, a must.

UV bulbs eventually lose effectiveness and need to be updated every 6 months. You may get a UV meter to precisely monitor the lamp's radiation if you wish to be in the cautious zone.

Mercury Vapor Lamps

You may use mercury vapor lamps for a grownup dragon tank, which combines heat and the whole spectrum of sunshine. Due to their heat potential, you will need to utilize special ceramic casings for these lights. They often have an exquisite appearance and are adjustable in height.

Although some people find the configuration more practical and attractive than the two-beam component solutions we previously mentioned, it is important to remember that all of this raises the cost of the system.

We must emphasize that the science of UV lamps and optimum terrarium illumination is a vast subject.

3.3 The Heating Equipment: Optimal Tank Temperature

Beardies live in the desert, as you well know. That indicates that they like hot weather, but not only hot weather. It also implies that they require a thermal gradient, with a hot place beneath the basking light and a cold area in the contrary direction.

An extended tank rather than a rectangular one will assist you in providing the gradient and lighting.

The area where you will be basking should be 110°F or higher. Even at nighttime, the ambient temp must never drop below 70°F. Although other sources state 65°F, We would rather choose the side of caution.

In the majority of households, the temp doesn't drop below this point. However, if your beardie's room temperature falls below 70°F, you must purchase an undertank warmer to maintain the proper temperature.

Because undertank warming provides a more natural kind of nocturnal heat than ceramic bulb warming, it is better suitable for this use. Stones heated by the sunlight during the day emit that warmth at night, but from below.

3.4 Kind Of Substrate Best For Bedding

Everyone believes you must never put a young beardie on any sandy substrate, even if opinions on older dragons and habitats vary.

Though why?

Well, young beardies eat quite enthusiastically and energetically. They might assault their prey so quickly and fiercely that they could ingest the substrate, resulting in bowel impaction or other terrible and hazardous health issues.

The second problem is that dragons have a lot of feces, which makes it difficult to keep the substrate clean in the tank.

Let's quickly go through the different kinds of substrate you may use for your dragons.

Non- Preferable Substrate: Wood Shavings, Coconut Coir, Sand

Preferable Substrate: Paper Towels, Newspaper, Vinyl Tiles, Slate, Ceramic Tiles, Reptile Carpets

Newspaper is perhaps the least expensive and most readily accessible throwaway ground cover for the bearded dragon's aquarium. Most newspapers readily absorb liquids, which is advantageous since it prevents the muck from spreading throughout the tank. The material is also durable, so as your pet becomes active, it won't slide off beneath his feet. Always wait a few weeks before placing newly printed newspapers inside a cage by leaving them out in the open. By doing so, you may be certain that the publishing paint is dried & won't seep.

Another popular throwaway material is **paper towels**. They are much simpler to replenish than newspapers and seem cleaner and neater. These are more effective in absorbing liquids. They are typically utilized in aquariums for young animals.

The most contentious substrate for lizards kept in desert vivaria is **sand**. On the bright side, sand is beautiful and said to be the most organic material for vivariums in desert environments. Sand may and will result in impaction if it is unintentionally consumed by your lizard, which is a major drawback. Additionally, it might be more difficult to maintain cleanliness, encouraging the growth of unwelcome microbes, which raises the risk of illness.

Despite all the dangers, if you still want to put sand, you must replace it monthly and remove the dirty portions daily. To reduce the possibility of accidentally ingesting the substrate, serve your beardie on a flat surface like a plate or clean plastic lid.

Young dragons shouldn't be exposed to sand since they are ravenous feeders and will almost certainly end up with a significant amount of sand in their stomachs, which may kill them. Unlike their younger counterparts, adult dragons prefer to pick food up with tongues instead of driving their whole teeth into it.

While **coconut coir** has excellent anti-microbial qualities, beardies should not use it. Coconut coir is not ideal for a sandy vivarium since it prefers to retain water and is a loose substrate that increases the danger of impaction. Remember that respiratory illnesses may result from excessive wetness.

The solution to the **wooden shavings** problem is straightforward: they should never be used in terrariums. In addition to being unusual for beardies and other lizards, it may include chemicals and, if not properly digested, result in impaction. Therefore, adding wood shavings to any bearded dragon tank is a major no-no.

Vinyl tiles have grown in popularity as a terrarium material. They are inexpensive, available in various colors, and simple to cut. They're non-porous, allowing you to easily wipe feces and moisture off the surface. Vinyl, though, is not flawless. It is finer than stone slate and gives your reptile less grip. Potential problems with PVC are also beginning to emerge as the harmful health impacts of plastic are explored more in-depth. Because the base of the terrarium will be warmed, plastic may allow dangerous substances to seep out. Given what we have learned about human habitation, We would much rather choose the path of caution even if no study is done to confirm or disprove this in a conservatory context.

The polished **ceramic tiles** in your toilet spring to mind first when you consider ceramic tiles. However, many designs and patterns seem to be in the marketplace, including some resembling gravel and stone. Other benefits of ceramic tiles abound as well. They are quite cheap and simple to cut. Additionally, animals often like the notion that tiles will warm up. However, if your lamp generates a significant amount of heat, this is the sole feature with which you need to exercise extreme caution. It would help if you didn't place tile or rock slates beneath the basking area.

The most aesthetically pleasing and authentic-looking floor covering on the ranking is **slate**. It also has other great properties. It gives the lizard a solid grip for locomotion and shortens his nails. Beardies like the heat they exude when it heats up well. Slate, though, has a few drawbacks as well. Compared to alternatives like ceramic tiles and vinyl, it is more difficult to cut. The second problem is that it is more porous, so that it will collect excrement and other contaminants more readily. It requires more thorough washing and bleaching to avoid stinking and retaining germs.

Although **reptile rugs** are often utilized in bearded dragon habitats, they're generally short-lived. Beardies rapidly get filthy since they urinate often and everywhere. If you purchase a reptile carpet, choose one fiber loop-free and dragon-friendly. Beardies risk injury if their lengthy claws or fingers get caught there.

There are always hobbyists ready to take up the dangers associated with loose substrates. Some fans are enthusiastic about a perfect replica of the species' original environment. Some pet owners dislike seeing their animals dissatisfied when there is nowhere for them to burrow or dig because they wish to promote natural behavior.

If you fall into this category, you might consider utilizing a bioactive substrate similar to a desert in your bearded dragon vivarium.

It should be capable of holding air and moisture so that it may serve as a home for the bacteria and other small invertebrates that aid in the organic breakdown of terrarium waste. It is, in fact, bioactive because of this.

A bioactive substrate may also support the growth of plants. If the coating is dense enough, it will maintain its structure and allow your creature to make tunnels rather than continue to dig aimlessly. Biologically active substrates still run the danger of compacting, however. It is ideal for each owner to determine this for themselves based on their particular bearded dragon's personality, state of health, and food preferences.

Hydration is another problem with this kind of substrate; because bioactive substrate requires moisture to perform its duties, you will have to keep a closer eye on the terrarium's moisture to ensure it doesn't rise over acceptable levels.

3.5 Accessories And Decorations For Bearded Dragons

Decorated features serve significant purposes in every vivarium, allowing your creatures to bask, relax, and conceal their innate requirements and instincts. Bearded dragon tanks need several things.

- Placing a wood or boulder in a heated area

- Climbing branches and hammocks

- A little hiding area; paving stones make excellent and simple ones

Basking Architecture

Like most other diurnal reptiles, bearded dragons like sunbathing. Give them somewhere to rest, such as a log directly beneath the spotlight or a rock arrangement. But watch out for overheating, particularly if the surface is made of stone, which may absorb a significant amount of heat. You may avoid this by choosing the proper light intensity and determining the proper distance from the bathing area.

Hammocks And Branches For Climbing

All beardies like climbing as a different preferred pastime. Their native environments are where the climbing behavior is seen as well. They can enjoy the sun, keep an eye out for intruders, and hunt for food when seated in a high position. Because of this, your pet will happily hang around in the terrarium environment and above ground.

Bearded dragons usually prefer sturdy, spotless branches. Specially made hammocks are yet another comfort the pet sector has to provide. They might also be created at home. Once they acclimate to them, most pets find them cozy and like lounging around.

Hiding Spots

Concerns about bearded dragons adopting caves and other concealment have been raised on several sites. The concern is legitimate since they need a lot of UV radiation to be healthy.

However, hiding is a normal response for all animals, particularly for creatures who are being hunted. A lizard lacking a hiding spot will always be under stress.

Another reminder that healthy, energetic dragons are like basking in the sun. Instead of taking away your beardie's hiding area if he spends a lot of time hiding, one should attempt to figure out why. Is he eating consistently? Are there any symptoms of a disease? Has your alteration in his environment caused him stress, or are you touching him too much?

If you've identified the causes of your dragon's excessive concealment but still think the habit is keeping him from healing, you may construct a shallower, smaller cave out of pavement tiles that might cover roughly half of his length. He will utilize the UVB light that will continue to be reflected from the remaining half of his tail and back.

Do I Need To Take My Beardie For A Walk?

Despite what you may have seen online and on Video content, beardies do not yearn for a journey to a faraway place or a park.

In our forthcoming chapter on behavior and health, we'll go into further detail on this subject. You must understand that these dragons need sunlight in a safe, pesticide and predator-free environment to walk about, soak up the rays, and perhaps nibble on some dandelions. The ideal location would be your home backyard, where you would have complete control.

Proper Walking Techniques For Bearded Dragon

The following tips will help you start bringing your bearded dragon outside:

- Never release a beardie that isn't old enough or used to handling.

- Start cautiously by bringing your beardie to a predetermined spot for short durations.

- Only bring the beardy outdoors when the temperature is appropriate—as warm as the midpoint in their tank. Never remove them from the tank when damping is over 65 percent, or the shade's temperature is lower than the lowest setting. Always wait till it is sunny outside.

- Refrain from taking these trips every day.

- You will eventually be able to gauge your beardie's disposition. Some are introverted by nature as compared to others. After each "picnic," keep an eye out for symptoms of stress, like skipping food and drink or spending a lot of time hiding.

Your pet should have a cover, such as a bench or other similar roofed structure, that he may hide beneath when he is frightened. It's also a good idea to use a harness. Bearded dragon harnesses are available for purchase or may be made quite easily at home.

- If your reptile exhibits discomfort, stop the walk and return him to his environment.

- Never combine your pet with other animals, even if you think they won't hurt him.

Should I Provide My Beardie With A Feeding Tank?

It was once recommended to feed bearded dragons in a dedicated feeding tank because of their propensity for being messy and to prevent sand impaction problems.

The discomfort your beardie can experience due to this feeding approach is the main reason it must be avoided.

Young bearded dragons are particularly vulnerable to stress. You are undoubtedly aware that a freshly purchased beardie takes some time to become acclimated to his new cage after being placed there. They sometimes spend days refusing to consume or leave their home.

The trauma of new habitat is repeated every time you move your pet to a new cage to feed. Since they are easy pickings for larger predators in the wild, young beardies are more wary and tense than adults.

Even while adult beardies are less timid than young ones, they nevertheless prefer to eat in their familiar surroundings.

In the end, ensuring that your primary cage is secure for feeding is preferable, devoid of sand or tiny cracks that feeder insects may penetrate.

3.6 Can Bearded Dragons Coexist With Other Lifeforms?

By nature, bearded dragons live alone. To make housing simpler or just because individuals like having more than 1 pet, they often keep many pets together in confinement or cages with different species. There are many crucial guidelines you must adhere to if you do this:

- The initial step is having a big enough cage equipped with adequate hideout and basking spots to meet the requirements of all pets.

- If your habitat is exceptionally roomy, roughly twice the size of the preferred place for a lone beardie (which translates to 200 gallons), We wouldn't advocate keeping more than 2 animals in each tank or 3 if your cage is truly big.

- A backup tank to split your animals is essential if anything goes wrong.

- Be aware that beardies may sometimes eat smaller lizards. To prevent the predatory urge from being triggered, roommates' beardies need to be identical in size.

- Two males should never live together because they will battle over territory. The least stressful alternative for having two beardies is to keep 2 females.

Some intrepid enthusiasts attempt to maintain several kinds of lizards together. The fact that these share the same size and originate from similar or very comparable environments is crucial.

As you can see, there's no precise protocol for the ideal arrangement for this dragon regarding the kind of substrate, decorations, tanks, and Hammocks.

As you keep an eye out for your pet's safety and fundamental requirements, you may mix what matches your tastes and demands. Your beardie will have all he needs to flourish in a warm, dry, well-lit habitat with both UVB/UVA and visible wavelengths, secure and pleasant.

Chapter 4: Purchasing A Bearded Dragon

Bearded dragons, sometimes known as "beardies," are calm, docile reptiles that need little maintenance. For kids over 5, these animals make wonderful pets since they need little upkeep. To purchase a beardie, you need first choose a suitable dragon that fits your demands as a pet owner & your wallet. The pet is then available for purchase through a registered breeder, in a pet shop, or at a reptile exhibit.

4.1 Choosing Your Bearded Dragon

Go for a fully-developed dragon. Although young dragon babies are adorable to look at, they're vulnerable and more likely to become sick. Some newborns may also outgrow their desire to eat and need force feeding to survive. A fully developed or almost fully grown dragon may be kept as a pet & will be robust and simple to care for.

- Seek for a lizard between six to ten weeks old and six to ten inches long. This will guarantee that the lizard is developed and is not too immature. Before you purchase the beardie, you may also inquire with the breeder regarding her age. Choose a beardie of the same gender if you currently own one & are hoping to add to your collection. Normally, 2 female dragons get on well nicely. A female and male dragon can mate or engage in combat, which might result in unwanted dragon offspring in your vivarium. You may wish to refrain from purchasing more than 1 beardie at once since they can eventually get along badly. Then you'd have to sell one or create individual vivariums for each dragon.

- Verify the bearded dragon's alertness and weight. As you visit the dragon's cell and she seems awake and attentive, watch to see if she turns her gaze towards you. The dragon shouldn't seem listless or have eyes that are sunken in since these traits might indicate disease or dehydration. Additionally, make sure the dragon's face is free of fluid or pus by inspecting it. It would help if you watched to see whether the dragon seems fat and big. Check on her tail and limbs. A robust reptile should have enough fat in its tail, which is where lizards store fat.

- Check to see whether the dragon has any skin or limb breaks. Please make sure the dragon's skin is free of blemishes, sores, and irritated pimples by inspecting it. Then check her toes, tail, or limbs to ensure the skin isn't damaged or swollen-looking. Verify the dragon is bone-free since shattered bones may indicate a metabolic bone disorder. As these may also be metabolic, degenerative disease symptoms, you should check her toes and limbs to ensure they don't twitch or shake. You may watch the dragon move about in the cage to ensure she can use most limbs effectively. When moving, the dragon shouldn't stutter or limp. Even though they won't grow back, broken toes or the base of the tail are acceptable since they often mend on their own. Broken ribs and injured arms or legs, however, are hardly encouraging signs.

- Verify the hygiene of the enclosure. You must check the dragon's enclosure to ensure it looks well-kept and has clean water and food. You must ensure the dragon is receiving adequate UVB light in its habitat and that supplements have been provided to it.

4.2 Purchasing A Bearded Dragon

- Purchase your beardie from a breeder. Reliable reptile breeders sell beardies to many lizard enthusiasts. The safest alternative is often to get from a breeder since many specialize in raising one breed, reducing the risk of sickness, harm, and disease. You may locate bearded dragon caregivers online and via your regional herpetological organization.

- Bearded dragon prices might vary from pet breeder; however, they typically range from $100 to $200 per creature. Check the cages in which the beardies are kept for cleanliness whenever you tour the breeder. Ensure you thoroughly examine the dragon's anatomy and demeanor to ensure he will make a healthy pet.

- Buy a lizard from a pet shop. A lizard may also be purchased at your neighborhood pet shop, albeit it might be more challenging to guarantee its health. The optimal choice is to get from a breeder; however, if you cannot contact one, you may only purchase from a pet shop. Look for a pet shop where the same breed is kept in the same habitat. You should carefully check the dragon before buying him, as well as check the cage for hygiene.

- Attend reptile exhibits to look for dragons. They may also be purchased at reptile fairs or other gatherings where breeders and collectors gather to trade reptiles. Ensure the enclosure housing the dragons is tidy and well-maintained. You must also speak with the producer at the event to confirm that the beardies have received the required vitamins and UVB exposure. A trustworthy breeder may concentrate on raising one specific kind of bearded dragon.

4.3 Welcoming Your Dragon Home

- Set up and prepare the cage. You must have your new dragon's cage prepared and set up before bringing it home. For one beardie, you need a terrarium that is 23 inches high, 47 inches long, and 23 inches broad. More than 1 dragon may be kept inside the same vivarium or cage, but it has to be big enough for that many.

- The enclosure needs to include glass sides and a screen top for ventilation. The substrate that is safe for reptiles should be put at the base. Include climbing surfaces for your new pet, like branches and rocks, and hiding spots in the enclosure. Concerning the safest ground for a reptile cage, there is significant debate. Even sand that is harmless for reptiles may result in a gut impaction.

Examining the benefits and drawbacks of various substrates is essential to choose which is right.

- Use a UVB light, a 10 - 12 % fluorescent, to ensure the cage is warm and comfy. It would help if you also had a colder, shady end of the terrarium with temperatures between 22 to 26 ° C. The tank's humidity level ought to be low.

- Expect the beardie to be apprehensive or shy. The initial few days in its new home with you may cause your pet to exhibit cautious or anxious behavior. During the first 2 to 3 days, she might not eat adequately while she adjusts to her new surroundings. She should start eating regularly and become less reserved after getting used to you & her new habitat.

- To strengthen your relationship with your dragon, establish a routine for handling it. For her to become accustomed to being handled and caressed, try to hold her routinely. Also, use your hands to gently pick her up and hold her four limbs. You should only touch her for 10 - 15 minutes to avoid lowering her core temperature.

- Establish a food regimen for the dragon. To help your pet acclimate to scheduled mealtimes, attempt to get her up on a feeding plan as soon as possible. Due to their voracious nature, bearded dragons consume living animals, plants, and invertebrates. Your pet should be fed once a day, ideally in the morning, to let her digest her meal throughout the day.

Chapter 5: Bearded Dragon Nutrition And Diet

Have you heard that the food you choose for your beardies has to be carefully considered? A few typical human meals are poisonous to them! In this chapter, you may learn about the ideal food for bearded dragons:

The most common pet lizard nowadays is the beardies, as we all affectionately refer to it. You might believe feeding beardies is simple since they are omnivores, meaning they consume insects and a broad range of plant items. But let's not draw any quick judgments.

Do you realize that there are popular human meals harmful to beardies? Therefore you need to be very cautious while choosing staple foods for them. Their diet also has to vary as they get older and mature.

There are still many unanswered issues, particularly given the widely divergent advice you may encounter in pet stores and online.

Do bearded dragons consume meat? Do they need to eat a lot of vegetables or not? Which vitamin pills are best for them?

We've done extensive research on bearded dragon dietary practices to assist you, and We've put all that information into this potentially informative chapter.

5.1 What Do Beardies Consume In The Wild?

Beardies are opportunistic, omnivorous predators in the wild. This implies that they'll consume whatever prey they catch, most notably insects. However, they will consume varying amounts of the available greens.

It is impossible to completely duplicate their diverse diet in confinement, but it is unnecessary.

To provide your pet with a healthy meal, a variety of readily accessible insects, vegetables, leafy greens, & occasional fruit will be more than sufficient.

What Else Can Beardies Eat As Pets?

A balanced meal of insects and suggested plant stuff is best for bearded dragon pets. Breeders often add a biweekly pinkie mouse. However, this must be done with care.

Most of the food consumed by young and baby beardies would be animal protein; however, as they become older and mature, they must consume more plant food.

5.2 Ratio Of Plant To Insect Food

There are two camps of thought regarding the animal and plant meal proportion that beardies should eat.

In several publications, the most prevalent recommendation is that:

Young adult dragons should transition to a 50: 50 diet; adult beardies must eat the reverse of what infants do, 20 to 30% of insects & 70to 80percent of plant materials, while baby dragons must consume roughly 80 percent of insects while 20 percent of plant items.

This advice is based on a reasonable premise: because adult dragons are less energetic in captivity than in the wild, they must consume less fatty foods to prevent obesity, which is a problem for bearded dragons kept in terrariums.

Even yet, some animal owners suffer when their animal begins to refuse this diet dominated by plants, which appears to be a regular occurrence.

On the contrary, other publications advise feeding a dragon 75 percent insect protein throughout its existence.

A narrative from the little scientific study on the nutrition of wild beardies supports this idea. Only 16 percent of the wild-caught animals' total gastrointestinal tract discovered during the inspection was made up of plant stuff. Insects made up 61 percent of the total. The remainder comprised pebbles, various trash, and a few skink bones. "A meal of multiple insect species, complemented with green vegetables, might be the most approximate diet of P. vitticeps.

However, it is a reality that domesticated animals are significantly less energetic than their wild counterparts.

That is the initial source of the suggestion for a diet high in plants.

If your mature beardie enjoys eating vegetables, a diet high in plants will be perfect for him.

If you avoid high-fat staples like mealworms & allow your beardie some opportunity to walk, however, think that if your beardie exhibits mostly carnivorous instincts, balancing the plant-animal diet ratio to roughly 1:1 won't hurt him either.

You may decide what you think will be ideal for your pet, depending on all the data available to you.

5.3 Which Insects Are Edible To Bearded Dragons?

Almost any frequently grown commercial insects may be given to them as food:

Staple:

- Roaches

- Crickets

- Locusts

Regular:

- Silkworms

- Super worms

- Hornworms

- Calci-worms

- Mealworms (rarely to adults)

Treats Only:

- Waxworms

- Butterworms

Only wax worms and mealworms, which have the greatest amount of fat on the checklist, shouldn't be consumed as a treat and must be avoided.

It is well known that dragons will happily consume canned and dried insects made specifically for reptiles. Nevertheless, We would only suggest this as a dish for special occasions or emergencies. To properly satisfy their dietary requirements, bearded dragons must consume live insects.

5.4 Which Plants Are Edible To Bearded Dragons?

According to nutritional studies and the beardie's native diet, your dragons' basic plant foods should be:

- Alfalfa

- Dandelion greens

- Escarole

- Mustard

- Endive

- Collard

5.5 Which Vegetables And Fruits May Be Eaten By Bearded Dragons?

You'll often add veggies to your beardie's everyday meals around 4 times a week to offer variety and extra nutrition. The following vegetables are often suggested for your beardies:

- Peas

- Squash

- Green beans

- Bell pepper

- Cucumber

The following fruit may be used occasionally or as a garnish to make the green salad more appetizing:

- Pears

- Apples

- Strawberries

- Mango

- Blueberries

- Grapes

5.6 Diet Of Juvenile & Baby Bearded Dragons

Regarding the appropriate food for young and newborn bearded dragons, everyone is at least in agreement. Eighty percent of it should consist of insect feeds, while the remaining twenty percent should be of plant material, mostly leafy greens and some fruit.

Baby and young beardies eat a much because of their fast development. 3 to 4 feedings each day are recommended. Give them as much food as they consume in five to ten minutes.

Baby dragons must consume everything of an adult dragon's food but in lesser portions. Use tiny mealworms that have recently shed their skins, as well as tiny roaches and crickets. Add chopped fruits, vegetables, and greens.

Ensure to add greens as the primary source of plant nutrition since if you start them on it when they're young; they won't have any trouble taking it when the percentage of greens in their diet rises.

Why Isn't My Baby Beardie Eating? Now What?

Finding out why your young dragon isn't eating is the initial thing you must do if this is the case.

- Being held leads to stress in baby dragons, so stress is a typical cause of food refusal. When holding them often, you should wait until they are a maximum of 5 to 10 inches tall.

- If you've been feeding your animals from a different tank, stop. Although some animals may tolerate this approach, most will find it distressing to have their habitat changed with each meal.

- Verify the tank's temp. It must reach 105°F under the resting light to guarantee appropriate metabolism.

- A lot of newborn beardies are picky eaters when it pertains to vegetables. Try mixing some worms into the leafy salad to encourage them to eat the greens while pursuing the worms.

- Immediately swap out any loose substrate you might be using with a paper towel, and keep an eye out for any symptoms of impaction. Some occurrences of food rejection may be caused by ingesting substrate and the ensuing impaction.

5.7 Mineral And Vitamin Supplements

Even with a diversified diet, your beardies still need minerals and vitamins to be healthy. To prevent overdose, vitamins must be taken with care.

Let's look at some of the key reservations people have about supplements.

Calcium

The majority of commercially reared feeder insects seem to be calcium deficient. Regarding greens, various plants may have varying capacities for absorbing calcium. Because of this, calcium is a necessary supplement for the beardie, and you must dust your insects with it 5 times a week for grownups and every day for little dragons.

Because the powder won't wash off the greens as quickly as insects, some advise dusting salads instead of insects; we urge you to attempt this strategy, but if it increases your aversion to consuming greens, adhere to insects.

Ratio Of Phosphorus To Calcium

It is crucial to constantly aim for a phosphorus-to-calcium ratio of 1:1 for appropriate metabolism. You'll see that many items, notably feeder insects, get an uneven P: Ca ratio if you read the nutritional tables. Because of this, calcium supplements are even more crucial.

Vitamin D3

Your beardies will require adequate amounts of vitamin D3 to process calcium. One reason diurnal lizards bathe so frequently is that vit D3 is a substance the body produces when it is subjected to sunshine.

To compensate for the absence of direct light exposure in the habitat, you must provide a UVB lamp. Additionally, you need to occasionally take your pet outdoors so he may enjoy the sunshine.

It's debatable if supplementing bearded dragons with vitamin D3 is a good idea. There are many allegations that beardies cannot effectively use vitamin D3 via supplements, & some research suggests that these assertions may be accurate. If your beardie never gets exposure to sunlight outdoors, supplement calcium with D3 to meet his nutritional requirements. Don't provide these supplements to the feeding insects every day.

Iron

Your beardie's diet may be low in iron. It's a little complicated when it comes to iron. Many green leafy vegetables, including spinach, collards, and kale, have healthy quantities and significant levels of harmful oxalates. Also, since there is a chance of overdosing, iron supplements should not be used excessively.

The easiest way to ensure he gets enough iron is to include a little quantity of palatable dark leafy greens, like kale, in his diet, along with a weekly supplement.

Never add red meat to your pet's food to increase the iron content.

Vitamin A

Beta-carotene, a type of vitamin A, is often found in numerous vegetables & leafy greens. Beta-carotene is transformed into vitamin A in the body as required, and any extra is eliminated.

However, the body cannot keep synthetic vitamin A in this form. Your beardie may get poisoned by vitamin A if he already receives all the vitamin A he requires from other synthetic supplements.

Use reptilian multivitamins that are low in vitamin A or include beta-carotene rather than the synthetic kind to remain safe. Avoid feeding your bearded dragon anything rich in vitamin A on the same day you dust food with vitamin powder.

What Should I Feed My Bearded Dragon?

These noteworthy guidelines and advice can help you nurture your beardie.

- Never give your beardie anything to eat bigger than the area between their eyes. This is crucial since feeding bigger insects or vegetables may result in major health problems, including paralysis, loss of motor function, gastrointestinal impaction, or even mortality.

- Consistently give your dragon new food. The only way to guarantee that your dragon's meals include the right amount of nutrients and water is to provide live insects & fresh plants.

- Fresh, thoroughly rinsed, coarsely diced plant food is always best since the leaf moisture will continue to hydrate your bearded dragon.

- Have your bearded dragon's first feeding take place 2 hours after turning on the lamps, and its final feeding takes place 2 hours after turning them off. To properly digest their meal, they must be warm.

- You can give your beardie special tweezers or let them seek their prey instinctively. It will keep them occupied and in excellent condition to let them pursue the prey around; however, having tweezers on board is useful if you need to feed manually for whatever reason. • Always serve prey in a feeder dish if the habitat has a loose substrate. Impaction brought on by swallowing the substrate may result in difficult medical treatments and even deaths.

- When your dragon stops eating, empty his tank of the leftover food. Don't hold onto it for later.

- Generally speaking, you may provide insects 6 days a week in varying amounts. Offer vegan options only on the 7th day. Four days each week should be reserved for vegetables.

The amount your beardies should eat is a constant source of discussion. Some suppliers even provide whole diets with the proper amount of veggies and feed insects.

But in our opinion, you need to feed your reptile as much as he can consume. Reptiles don't have cognitive issues that result in food cravings, and binge eating as other pets (or people) do. He will finish once he is satisfied.

Obesity should not be a concern as long as you provide him with the suggested meals in the right portions.

For beardies, the recommended food schedule is 4 meals for the young, followed by 3 meals. Feeding them once or twice each day is OK when they are older. Even though when they carry eggs, females, whether infertile or fertile, might not feel like eating, so they should consume at least two meals daily.

Bearded Dragons' Method Of Water Ingestion

Due to their dry origins, beardies have adapted to get most water from their diet, particularly juicy plants. But they should always have access to clean drinking water in a tray.

Many beardies will entertainingly soak themselves inside the water tray if it is large enough. Since the activity is among their rehydration techniques, this shouldn't be criticized.

The only drawback to taking these regular baths is that they frequently prompt bowls to urinate in the water, which is beneficial for their digestion but not particularly great for your to-do list.

It may be required to change the water more than once a day occasionally, but if doing so makes your life simpler, your beardie is likely content and healthy.

When your beardies seem stiff or picky about feeding or unsure whether he is receiving sufficient water from his meal, you may and should sometimes give him a warm dip outside the habitat. He will benefit from soaks to stay hydrated, unwind their muscles, and aid digestion.

Additionally, beardies like sprinkling, and it will lick the dew off of their snout and the aquarium glass. Just be careful not to increase the moisture in your desert tank while sprinkling.

Every time you feel like they could need a drink, you may dab a small amount of water on his nose. It's a good way to strengthen your relationship with your pet.

Your bearded dragon may not be eating for a variety of reasons. Some are alarming, including sickness, digestive problems, constipation, or stress. Others are natural, such as habituating to new surroundings or the periodic resting time known as brumation.

If the following conditions are present in addition to the lack of appetite, consult a vet:

- Digestive issues
- Lethargy
- Skin issues like incomplete shedding

- Injuries and wounds

- Bloat

5.8 FAQs About Bearded Dragons Nourishment & Nutrition

Can bearded dragons eat an apple?

Yes. Apples are completely safe for reptiles like beardies to consume. They are abundant in vitamins like vitamin C and offer adequate hydration.

Are Bananas edible to bearded dragons?

Yeah, but not often. Bananas are somewhat low in the water and highly packed with sugar.

Are blackberries edible to bearded dragons?

Yup. You may periodically give your beardie blackberries. Don't forget to start with a tiny dose to monitor digestion.

Can bearded dragons eat blueberries?

Yup. Blueberries may be served as a special treat sometimes, much as blackberries.

Are Cantaloupes edible to bearded dragons?

Yes. You can sometimes give your beardie cantaloupe. Vitamin A content is high.

Are grapes edible to bearded dragons?

Yup. You may sometimes offer grapes as a reward. Additionally edible and a healthy complement to the meal are grape leaves.

Are raisins palatable to bearded dragons?

No. Raisins are dried, and their sugars are highly concentrated, in contrast to grapes, which are high in water. Don't give them to your bearded dragon.

Do beardies eat kiwi?

In principle, yes, but we would steer clear of it due to the excessive oxalate and acidity levels.

Do bearded dragons eat mangoes?

You may give your beardies the extra bit of unripe mango. Mango is rich in vitamin A and relatively high in oxalates.

What about oranges for bearded dragons?

No. Oranges and other citrus fruits are not suitable for beardies to consume. The acidity is too high.

Are pears edible to bearded dragons?

Sure. Pears may be a staple fruit in your bearded dragon's menu. Prior to serving, cut them into tiny, thin pieces.

Can beardies eat strawberries?

Indeed, beardies can eat it as a fruit treat; they often like the luscious strawberries. Prior to serving, thoroughly rinse and finely cut them.

Do bearded dragons eat watermelons?

Indeed, sometimes feeding slices of watermelon to beardies is OK.

Is pineapple safe for bearded dragons to eat?

Yup, but only on rare occasions. Offer them cautiously to monitor the impact on the digestive system.

What about asparagus for bearded dragons?

Yes. One of the sporadic vegetables on your bearded dragon's menu may be asparagus. Offer him the plant's finely cut, top, more delicate portions.

What about avocados for bearded dragons?

Not at all. Avocados poison birds and reptiles. Although it is unknown exactly how much of this common fruit your

pet must consume to poison himself, you must never take a chance with even a single slice.

Is Bok choy safe for bearded dragons to consume?

Yeah, on occasion. But never consider bok choy a regular part of your diet.

Are Brussels sprouts safe for bearded dragons to consume?

Yeah, of course. Like all members of the cabbage family of plants, Brussels sprouts may be consumed in moderation.

Bearded dragons may eat carrots.

It would help if you chopped bearded dragons into very little circles. Carrots provide a lot of vitamin A and just a little bit of oxalates.

Bearded dragons can eat celery, right?

Yes. Celery leaves and sticks are equally edible to bearded dragons. It would help if you gave them a thorough wash & chop them correctly. Choose organic celery if you can because it is often excessively treated with pesticides.

Will chard nourish a bearded dragon?

Prevent it. Because chard contains a lot of oxalates, it must be handled similarly to spinach.

Bearded dragons may eat broccoli.

Yeah, beardies can sometimes eat steamed or fresh broccoli.

Are cucumbers edible to bearded dragons?

Yeah, on occasion. Although they are poor in nutrients, cucumbers are high in water, which is beneficial if your bearded dragon doesn't prefer to drink water straight from the container.

What about peas for bearded dragons?

Yes. Peas may be one of the most often consumed vegetables in your pet's diet, particularly snap peas and snow.

What about green beans for bearded dragons?

Yeah sure. Green beans and peas have the same characteristics.

Are green onions edible to bearded dragons?

No. Never give your lizard any onions, whether they are green or grown. They could be poisonous.

What about kale for bearded dragons?

Yes, but not often. Although kale is high in iron, calcium, and other beneficial elements, it also contains many oxalates, potentially harmful to bearded dragons if consumed in large numbers.

Are peppers edible to bearded dragons?

Yes. Rarely bearded dragons will consume delicious bell or red peppers. They have a lot of water & vitamin C but just a little bit of oxalates. Never give hot peppers to beardies.

Can bearded dragons consume potatoes?

No. Potatoes should never be eaten uncooked by bearded dragons. Although cooked potatoes are an alternative, they could potentially include toxins found in various potato plant sections. In contrast to humans, reptiles may be harmed by high concentrations.

Red cabbage is safe for bearded dragons to consume.

Yes, beardies may have a piece of cabbage once in a while, but it shouldn't become a regular food.

Can beardles eat spinach?

No. Spinach is not advised for beardies due to its high

oxalate content (which prevents calcium absorption) and regular pesticide treatment.

Are bearded dragons able to eat squash?

Yes. Beardies easily consume all varieties of squash, one of their favorite vegetables. Squash may also be used as a conversation starter for beardies who are wary about eating plant foods.

Can beardies consume mushrooms?

No. They contain excessive phosphorus, are difficult to digest, and certain mushrooms contain poisonous substances to beardies.

What about zucchini for bearded dragons?

Sure. Among the plant diets that are often suggested for beardies is zucchini. Remember that they contain a lot of phosphorus, so you should constantly balance them with calcium.

Do beardies eat greens?

No. Iceberg lettuce, which mostly includes fiber and water and a few other nutrients, is not advised as a diet for bears.

Mustard greens are edible to bearded dragons.

Among the daily green mainstays for beardies is advised to be mustard greens.

Arugula is safe for bearded dragons to consume.

Yes, you may sometimes give your beardie arugula, but please be mindful that it has a harsh flavor and is rich in vitamin A.

Do bearded dragons consume dandelion seeds?

Yes. One of the essential green foods in your pet's diet must be dandelions. Provide new leaves and the occasional fresh blossom top.

Do bearded dragons consume basil?

Yes. Basil may sometimes be provided and is acceptable for beardies to consume.

What about cilantro for bearded dragons?

Bearded dragons are safe to consume cilantro. Choose younger, simpler-to-digest leaves.

Do bearded dragons consume grass?

The grass is infamously hard to digest. Creatures that have adapted to rely on it for nourishment have very complex digestive systems. Eating grass has no advantages for either people or beardies.

You could see your bearded dragon chewing on grass if you allowed him to roam around the yard. Even while the odd grass munch shouldn't harm your animal, the habit shouldn't be promoted. In addition, your pet must only be permitted to wander in pesticide-free areas.

Earthworms are safe for bearded dragons to consume.

Yes, as a reward, but only for those specifically developed for this use. To prevent contact with parasites or other dangers, don't use bait store worms or those you pulled out yourself.

Can bearded dragons eat hornworms?

Sure. Hornworms are often suggested as a regular dietary source for pets. They are rich in water activity, have lower fat, and have an excellent calcium ratio. If you own a

pet that won't eat, try enticing him with such a hornworm since they are extremely green and often quite alluring to lizards.

Are mealworms edible to bearded dragons?

Yes, but only in moderation—especially about adult dragons. Although mealworms are a welcome treat for bearded dragons, they will not be their main source of nutrition. They are tougher to process than other species of larvae because they're fatty, have a low phosphorus-to-calcium ratio, and have relatively hard external shells.

However, feel free to feed juvenile beardies more of the just molted, white mealworms. Despite their drawbacks, they are the most straightforward feeder bug to produce at home. Thus every lizard keeper should keep a tiny colony on hand.

Are wax worms edible to bearded dragons?

Yeah, but only as a special treat. Wax worms are delectable and sought by lizards; however, they are too fatty to consume regularly. They may also be used as rewards for a beardie who has lost interest in food.

Are bearded dragons able to eat ants?

No. Ants are loaded with repulsive formic acid, which they also spit in self-defense. Most lizards in the environment may sometimes attempt to consume an ant, and only specialist lizard species, like horn lizards, can do so.

Are fireflies edible to bearded dragons?

No. For beardies, fireflies are very poisonous. Your beardies might perish if even one of them is devoured.

Are bearded dragons able to eat spiders?

No. Every spider carries a toxin in the glands of its fangs, and this poison might be harmful to your lizards. Don't give in to the urge to attempt feeding your bearded spiders.

Are beardies able to consume stink bugs?

No. Since stink bugs live up to their reputation, many attackers will avoid them. Stink bugs are possible pesticide transporters because of their high level of pesticide resistance as well as the possibility of burning from aromatic compounds. Always stay away from stink bugs.

Does the bearded dragon consume moths?

You may not go hunting for wild caterpillars for your beardie's food. Parasites, pesticides, and certain moths also contain protective compounds that might harm your pet. Additionally, they are not particularly nourishing.

Nevertheless, if your tank has a wire-mesh cover, a moth may come in, and your dragon will chase it and enjoy munching on it. Most of the time, there is no need for concern.

Do bearded dragons consume meat?

Never. While the precise effects of meat on the wellness of bearded dragons are unknown, it certainly includes too much fat and phosphorus, effectively preventing calcium absorption.

Additionally, giving your pet lizard uncooked meat raises the possibility that it could contract and later develop salmonella, which can harm you.

What about chicken for bearded dragons?

No. There hasn't been much study done on how chicken meat affects beardies. However, what We stated about other meats is also applicable to chicken.

Are bearded dragons fish eaters?

No. The effects of feeding fish to bearded dragons on their health have not been studied. Hence this is unknown. Beardies are unlikely to stumble across a trout in their native environment since they inhabit arid grasslands and deserts, meaning that fish is not their native meal.

Are eggs ingestible by bearded dragons?

Yes, but only sometimes. Eggs are an occasional fantastic addition to your dragon's normal diet because of their high nutritional density and the reality that omnivorous & carnivorous lizards unscrupulously graze on various eggs in their wild places. To reduce the chance of salmonella, serve them boiling.

Can beardies consume bread?

No. Bread will not be frequently fed to beardies or any other pet because of high sodium content, additives, & other substances. If your bearded creature requires medicine, it may be useful to conceal it.

Are there any plants that beardies should avoid eating?

A wide variety of plants poisons beardies. Thankfully, most animal owners wouldn't feed their animals with them, but they might come across them when pacing the residence or the backyard. The following is a list of typical plants that are poisonous to beardies:

- Horse Chestnut
- Oak
- Tulip
- Poppy
- Primrose

- Wisteria

- Milkweed

- Red Maple

Perhaps, you now understand how important it is to provide healthy food for your beardies.

If you do thorough research, it isn't difficult to accomplish either although. The majority of the things that bearded dragons should eat are readily accessible, so all you must do to get the idea of it is some practice and excellent preparation. You can quickly make the ideal beardie meal with the right expertise and information.

Conclusion

These wonderful, sun-loving dragons might be seen on the side of a road in the desert or hunting insects in a meadow in a forest. Similar to other Beardie species, this reptile strives to appear bigger and spikier than it is to any prospective predators by relying more on deception than bite.

Although Central Beardies are usually nocturnal, they are occasionally seen on highways after dark, particularly after warm days. This indicates that the animal might be more active at night than previously thought.

To maintain its ideal body temp, the beardies basks. They widen their jaws to varied degrees if their internal temperature is high and perhaps hazardous. This is likely done to allow the cooling effect from the wet mouth coverings to chill the blood flowing through the brain.

This type of Bearded Dragon is a skilled climber and is often seen perched on tree branches, stumps, rocks, and fence posts. The reptile will sunbathe in the sun and watch for prospective predators, prey, competitors, and partners from its high posture. They may spend much time sitting above land during very hot spells. For instance, a male once stayed mounted in the same tree, 3 meters high, for 3 weeks.

When startled, the lizard turns to confront the intruder with its mouth open & beard pushed out to accentuate its big jaw. The dragon swiftly inhales oxygen to enlarge the body, giving the impression that it is larger overall and that its spiky sides are unyielding.

The lizards can quickly change hue. One species, for instance, went from being almost yellow to nearly black in a matter of minutes. Males in their middle years often turn their bottom jaw from its natural color to black. The beard looks more impressive when inflated in a defensive posture.

Bearded dragons are calm, docile reptiles that need little maintenance. For kids over 5, these reptiles make wonderful pets since they need little upkeep. To purchase a beardie, you need first choose a suitable dragon that fits your demands as a pet owner & your wallet. The pet is then available for purchase through a registered breeder, in a pet shop, or at a reptile exhibit. However, Educating yourself about an animal's care requirements is crucial before bringing it into your home, as with any other animal.

Made in United States
Orlando, FL
28 June 2023

34589929R00070